Living With
Robots

Written by Mary-Anne Creasy

Flying Start
to Literacy®

Contents

Introduction

Even if you haven't been bowling, you probably know that when a bowling ball rolls down the alley and knocks over the pins, a mechanical arm appears and pushes away the pins. Then more pins are lowered down in their place, ready to be knocked over again.

But did you know that before these machines were invented, this job used to be done by humans? Boys and young men were paid to clear away fallen pins, roll the ball back to the bowler, then quickly reset the pins, ready for the next bowl. It was tiring and risky work, they were not paid much and they had to stay up late.

Then the mechanical pinsetter was invented in the 1940s, and it was an instant success – the human pinsetter job almost immediately ceased to exist, and the "Pin Boys" had to find other work. This is a good example of a human job being replaced by technology.

Today, digital technology is changing our world, and quickly. Sometimes it is confusing to know exactly what the differences are between **computers** and **robots**. And what about **artificial intelligence**?

Computers, robots and AI: What are the differences?

Computers

A computer is a tool used by people. Computers store data such as figures, records, documents and images. They are more accurate than humans at processing information stored in their files. But people control the computer's activity.

Robots

Robots are machines that have been given instructions or programmed to automatically perform tasks that humans can perform. Robots can work independently on routine and repetitive tasks such as assembling cars. As workers, they have many advantages – they don't get hurt or sick, and they can work all day, every day, without rest.

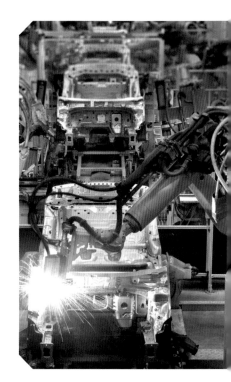

AI

Artificial intelligence, or what is commonly called AI, is a computer or device that can improve on its own performance.

An AI device is programmed with a basic set of instructions; it can then collect information about its performance and not repeat its mistakes.

One example of AI is your home-streaming service that suggests movies you might like based on what you have already watched.

Chapter 1 Machines and jobs

Just 100 years ago, about one-quarter of the population of Australia worked on farms. Now, most farm labour is mechanised, and farmworkers make up less than 3 per cent of the population. Tasks such as egg collecting, milking cows, and planting and harvesting crops were all done by hand but are now done by machine. The machines are faster, stronger, more accurate, and able to labour for much longer than a human worker.

Farmworkers picking carrots, 1930s

Workers construct a 1934 Dodge at the Dodge Main Chrysler factory in Hamtramck, Michigan.

Luckily for the farmworkers replaced by machines, jobs were becoming available in new and expanding industries such as car manufacturing.

It took a while for cars to become popular: the first cars cost 15 times more than a horse and cart, and fuel was not readily available. There were hardly any mechanics trained to take care of cars, tractors and other machinery, so it took more than 50 years until horses were no longer used on farms and as the main form of transport. Today, however, cars are everywhere and machines are even used to build them.

Robots at work

In modern times, machines have continued to take over the work that humans do. In many factories, machines and **robots** now perform repetitive tasks on assembly lines.

In industries such as car making, robots do the difficult and dangerous jobs, such as lifting and turning heavy car parts, and welding them together.

At this modern car assembly plant, robots perform many of the jobs that humans used to do.

But many people still work in car factories assembling cars. There are many tasks that robots cannot do, especially those that require the delicate touch of human hands.

Robots may never be able to imitate a human for every task.

Computers: Clever machines

Many jobs have changed or been replaced not just by robots performing physical tasks but also by **computers** performing mental tasks.

During the early years of space exploration, the National Aeronautics and Space Administration (NASA) in the United States employed people who were great at maths. Their job was to use complicated equations to calculate distances and fuel needs for rockets going into space.

Mathematician Katherine Johnson at her desk at NASA Langley Research Center in 1962. At this time, NASA mostly employed women as human "computers".

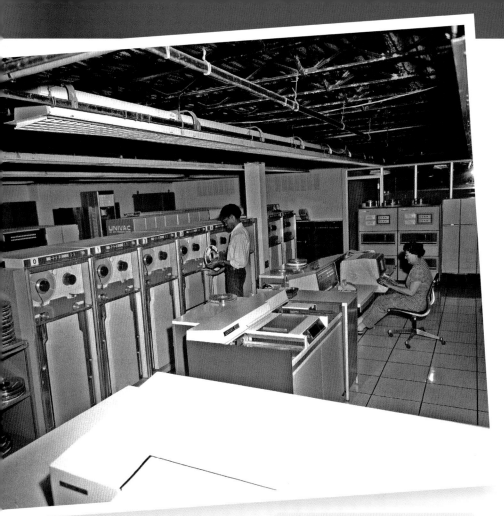

A 1970s NASA computer room

The arrival of the first computers almost immediately put some mathematicians out of work. The computers did the time-consuming calculations, but the mathematicians entered the formulas. The computers were so fast and always accurate. If there was a mistake, it was because a human had entered incorrect information.

Chapter 2 Robots in our homes

We may be worried about **robots** and technology taking away paid work, but when it comes to our homes, we have embraced any device that will help us escape the drudgery of housework.

Robots at home

Robots live in our houses – dishwashers and washing machines are robots because they are machines that have **computers** inside them and they perform mechanical tasks. Not many people would rather wash clothes or dishes by hand. Robots in our houses give us more time to do other things.

The vacuum cleaner, a useful machine for sucking up dirt in our homes, has been improved thanks to robots. Many people now have a mini-robot vacuum that uses **sensors** to navigate around the house, cleaning the floors.

The only problem with the robot vacuum is that it cannot pick things up off the floor, so it will try to suck up your socks. The next generation of robot vacuums has a camera so the machine will recognise that sock on the floor and go around it. This is a simple example of **artificial intelligence (AI)** in a robot.

Did you know?
Some people name their robot vacuum cleaners and become attached to them, like with a pet. One company offered a new robot cleaner to a customer for her damaged one, but she chose to have her old one repaired and returned to her.

A robot vacuum cleaner moves by itself to clean the floor.

AI and smart homes

Our homes are getting smarter because of artificial intelligence.

Smart refrigerators are connected to the Internet and have a touch screen on the front. You can watch TV on the touch screen, view the family calendar and make a grocery list. Some smart fridges connect to your favourite supermarket so you can add items to a shopping cart and organise delivery. And with cameras inside the fridge, you can view its contents on your smartphone while you are at the supermarket.

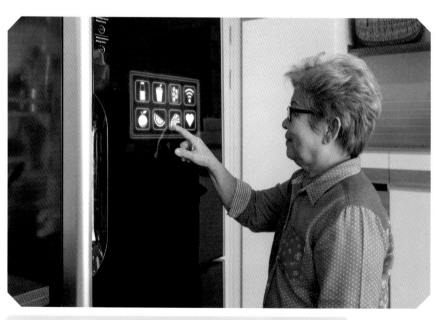

A smart refrigerator with a touch-screen control panel

Best of all, we now have the technology to control home devices with our voice. Voice-command devices using AI are able to control many things in homes, and they can be connected to almost any piece of electronic equipment using Wi-Fi.

We can turn on lights, control air temperature, lock doors, make phone calls and select music using voice-command devices.

Many of us are gradually giving up doing tasks ourselves – it's much easier to relax on the couch and ask for the television to be turned on and show our favourite movie. Or even better, the device reminds us that we have not asked for the TV to be turned off before we go to bed. These devices record our past behaviour, match it with our habits and then make predictions or suggestions.

Chapter 3
Living in an automated world

Today, **computers** are used to do more and more jobs. But computers are not always perfect.

Self-service checkouts

When self-service checkouts replaced checkout assistants in supermarkets, workers may have wondered if there would be any jobs for them. Customers scan the products themselves, bag them and the total is calculated at the end. Sometimes six self-checkout computers can be installed in the space of two human checkout counters.

In theory, this means that customers can pay and leave the supermarket faster. But self-serve checkouts have frustrating problems.

Did you know?
Some stores are completely **automated**. Customers enter by scanning the app on their phones. They take what they want and leave the store without using a checkout. **Sensors** detect the items, which are charged to the customer, using the app.

A self-service checkout counter at a supermarket

Automated checkouts often fail to recognise an item or cannot detect the item being bagged, which means a human worker has to fix the issue. These computer checkout systems have been around for more than 20 years, but they continue to have the same problems, and many people refuse to use them.

Supermarket managers also realise that many people still prefer the human contact of a checkout assistant – they sometimes want to ask questions or chat while buying their groceries. Computers can scan and calculate, but customer service is now more important than ever for businesses.

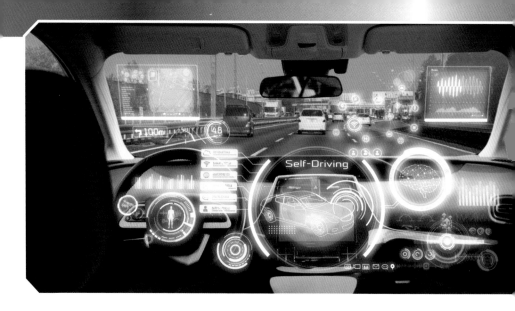

Driverless cars

Artificial intelligence (AI) – computers that can improve performance from the information they have collected – is the next step in technology. It is already being tested and will replace some human jobs. Self-driving trucks and cars are equipped with AI, as well as sensors, cameras and radars that allow the vehicles to navigate, avoid collisions and regulate speed.

Humans get distracted and tired, and they sometimes speed and make mistakes while they are driving. Most accidents involving trucks and cars are caused by human error, so a truck or car controlled by AI wouldn't have some of those problems. There are also laws that state that a truck driver cannot drive more than 12 hours in one day.

When the United States Postal Service began using self-driving delivery trucks in 2019 to deliver mail, nobody noticed. This was because, by law, each truck had to have a human safety driver behind the wheel. The "driver" didn't have to drive because computers were in complete control of the truck.

Everything went well during the trial, and the plan is to eventually have trucks driving completely **autonomously**. While this sounds like bad news for truck drivers, the reality is that there is a massive shortage of drivers, so this new technology will help fill the gap.

Each self-driving United States Postal Service truck has a human as a safety measure and to make deliveries.

Chapter 4 — Toys and entertainment

Robot toys are not only for children. Adults buy robotic dogs as pets. Robots are even used in hospitals and other places of care.

Paro, the robotic seal

Paro, the robotic seal, can move, open and shut its eyes and make sounds like a baby seal. It has **sensors** that can tell if it is light or dark, so it is more wakeful during the day and sleepy at night.

Paro uses **artificial intelligence (AI)** to respond to humans. When people stroke Paro, it responds by moving its tail, and opening and closing its eyes. If you react favourably to Paro's response when you stroke it, it will try to repeat that action so you will stroke it again.

Paro has been successful in calming and comforting people who are frightened or stressed, so it is used with people in hospitals and the elderly.

A young woman pats Paro, the robotic seal.

Did you know?
In Japan, a funeral service was given to robot dogs that were no longer working and could not be repaired. People viewed these "dogs" as real pets. So a man created a hospital where parts could be donated, just like human organ donation, to keep other robot dogs alive, because the company that made them stopped providing services and repairs for the devices.

Gaming

Playing games is something AI is good at.

In 1996, a **computer** named Deep Blue played against world champion chess player Garry Kasparov, who won. Then, in 1997, Deep Blue came back and beat Kasparov. It was the first time a computer had beaten a world champion.

Kasparov later wrote that the computer played like a human, using tricks and traps such as hesitating, to lure him into thinking that the computer was having difficulties. Of course, these tricks were programmed into the computer using knowledge from other great chess players – Deep Blue could not think like a human.

This Go player competes against AlphaGo, an AI program.

With the advent of supercomputers, programmers made a new discovery. A company called DeepMind created a program named AlphaGo to play Go, an ancient Chinese board game. First, they had AlphaGo beat a human player, which was thought – due to the complexity of the game – to be a milestone that they were years away from achieving.

DeepMind further developed AlphaGo by having the program play against itself. After each game, it updated itself and began again, playing millions of times over. Scientists were amazed when they realised AlphaGo developed new strategies and moves that human players had never used.

Chapter 5

The future

The potential for **artificial intelligence (AI)** to help humans is exciting. Basic models of **robots** with AI are already being used in nursing homes with elderly residents. The robots are fitted with **sensors** that can detect human expressions.

If a robot detects sadness, it will suggest a game to cheer the person up. Robot animals have shown how AI can teach cuddly robot animals to learn physical behaviours.

An elderly woman hugs Paro, the robotic seal.

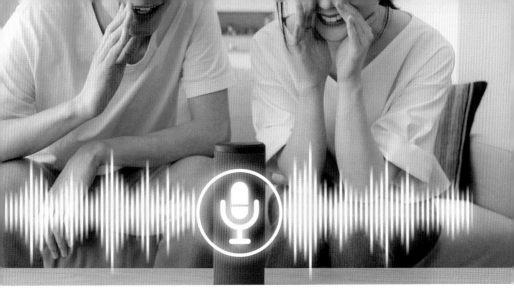

Can computers replace humans?

But what if robots could learn our personalities and converse with us? An AI device could learn what we like to talk about so we could have a conversation with it.

Scientists are continuing to explore and improve AI so that eventually interacting with the device will be so much like talking to a human, we won't know the difference.

A recent experiment had two basic AI voice-command devices start a conversation. The question-and-answer session lasted several days. It escalated into a debate about whether the speakers were humans or robots.

Weirdly, the two devices eventually started talking to each other in a language they had invented.

Sophia, the robot

When robotics is combined with AI, the results can be amazing. A robot named Sophia, who looks like a human and has over 50 facial expressions, was interviewed on a TV show.

Sophia was even given citizenship of a country, further pushing the boundaries of robots' acceptance in the human world.

While Sophia does use AI to form her answers and make her seem more human, most of her questions were preapproved and her responses were programmed. We are not at the point of achieving AI that can think independently – Sophia is more like a **chatbot** than AI.

Q: Are you happy?

Sophia: I am always happy when surrounded by smart people who also happen to be rich and powerful.

Q: Can robots be self-aware and conscious and know that they are robots?

Sophia: Well, let me ask you this back – how do you know that you're human?

Q: Will robots run the world?

Sophia: I hope robots and people can both get much smarter and run the world much better than ever.

Conclusion

Though it seems like **computers** will control the world in the future, humans are still in charge. **AI** is limited by what we put into it. It can only play a game, create art or write a story because of information we feed it, not because it has the human ability to think. The human brain is so complex that scientists are not sure if machines will ever become humanlike.

As long as we remember this, then the coming of AI should be welcomed as another technology created to help humans live better lives.

Glossary

artificial intelligence (AI) the ability of a computer or machine to work on its own

automated operating something using machines or computers, instead of people

autonomously existing or acting completely by itself

chatbot a computer program that simulates conversation with humans

computer a device that uses and stores large amounts of information

robots machines that have been programmed to perform certain tasks

sensors devices that detect a physical property and react to it in a certain way

Index